Open My Eyes

More Children's
Object Lessons

Kenneth A. Mortonson

CSS Publishing Company, Inc.
Lima, Ohio

OPEN MY EYES

Copyright © 1996 by
CSS Publishing Company, Inc.
Lima, Ohio

Library of Congress Cataloging-in-Publication Data

Mortonson, Kenneth, 1927-
    Open my eyes : more children's object lessons / Kenneth A. Mortonson.
      p.   cm.
    ISBN 0-7880-0566-9 (pbk.)
    1. Children's sermons. 2. Object-teaching. 3. Christian education—Teaching methods. 4. Christian education—Home training. 5. Christian education of children. I. Title.
BV4315.M657   1996
252'.53—dc20

                                          95-41492
                                            CIP

This book is available in the following formats, listed by ISBN:
0-7880-0566-9 Book
0-7880-0721-1 IBM 3 1/2 computer disk
0-7880-0722-X Macintosh computer disk

PRINTED IN U.S.A.

*This second volume is also dedicated
to my ten grandchildren.
They are representatives of the generation
whom we must teach in all corners of the world:*

*Michael and Nikolaus Wilim, living in Austria.
Christopher and Cathleen Mortonson, living in Massachusetts.
Eric, Adam, Aaron and Ryan Kline, living in Florida.
Michael and Andrew Mortonson, living in Wisconsin.
January 1995*

Table Of Contents

Author's Preface

These object lessons have been compiled over a period of 40 years as I have attempted to share the Word of God with people of all ages. I graduated from Northwestern University with a Bachelor of Science in Engineering degree. Out of this training of dealing with material things, I have always had an interest in how things work. Through the years I have also approached the objects of life with the question, "What lesson is illustrated by this object?" For example, a balloon will eventually burst when the pressure within exceeds the strength of the rubber. The lesson? Wise is the person who knows his or her own limitations and learns to live with them.

With this second volume, I have added an index of scriptural references. At the end of each lesson you will find a suggested passage of scripture that can be used as a background or a basis for the lesson. The new index will also enable you to find object lessons for use with specific passages.

I also hope that the experience of using this material will make it easier for you to see your own object lessons in life. Look for new meaning in the things you see and handle every day.

Open my eyes, that I may see Glimpses of truth Thou hast for me;
Place in my hands the wonderful key That shall unclasp, and set me free.
Silently now I wait for Thee, Ready, my God, Thy will to see;
Open my eyes, illumine me, Spirit divine!
(Clara H. Scott, 1895)

Introduction

As with the first volume, titled *That Seeing, They May Believe,* published in 1993, this book is dedicated to all who seek to teach the Christian faith. It is for parents, preachers, teachers and anyone else who is willing to take the time to endeavor to share the faith with the younger generation.

If you are willing to try using the material in your home life, remember that you will need to adapt the material to that setting. I suggest that you read these lessons and see what point is being made. Keep in mind that the written material is suggested for use in a group setting. Therefore, some modification may be necessary to adapt it to one child. Next, look at the possible times to use the illustration in the home found at the end of each lesson. See if you can think of other appropriate times when the setting might be right to share the object lesson with your child. Do this periodically and in the context of a prayer to God to help you find the right time and way to get the message across to the person you are seeking to help in the faith. Let your own creative spirit guide you in its use. Do not be afraid to use your own words as you use these symbols. I have shared with you what I see in these things and events, but you might see other applications. Let this experience sensitize you to the world of symbolism that surrounds you each day. Every part of creation has its own silent message waiting to be understood and shared. "The earth is the Lord's and the fulness thereof, the world and those who dwell therein" (Psalm 24:1).

Jesus pointed to common, everyday things as he taught the people. There were the lost coin (Luke 15:8), the mustard seed (Luke 13:18), houses built on rock and sand (Luke 6:47), and candles (Matthew 5:15), to mention just a few. One of the benefits of such a teaching approach is that whenever the symbol is seen or the event is experienced again, the lesson is quickly recalled. We teach children so that they will have basic Christian principles that they can apply to everyday living. Whatever helps them to remember these teachings will be of benefit to them.

True parental love seeks to affirm the infant with acts of kindness and concern that say to the child, "You are important to me, not because you have earned my love, but because you are a part of me and you are here." That parental love is unconditional. It is the ideal that also needs to be expressed within the Christian fellowship. All children are a part of the family of God. They are to be accepted, nurtured and loved. They are to be given their own special times to think about what it means to be a part of this family of God. They need to know they are important to the total body of believers. Seeking to communicate directly to them is one way of showing that commitment on the part of the Christian parents and the church adults.

For those who are teaching within the context of the church gathered, as you use the material in the formal setting of worship or the classroom, you will find that this type of instruction will also be beneficial to adults. Anything that can help people remember some of the basic concepts of the faith will be appreciated by them. Many members readily admit their lack of understanding when it comes to matters of faith. They are like the people to whom Paul wrote, "But I, brethren, could not address you as spiritual men, but as . . . babes in Christ. I fed you with milk, not solid food; for you were not ready for it" (1 Corinthians 3:1, 2). And Peter wrote, "Like newborn babes, long for the pure spiritual milk, that by it you may grow up to salvation; for you have tasted the kindness of the Lord" (1 Peter 2:2, 3).

The Christian journey is one that encourages continual spiritual growth. Our understanding of the teachings of our Lord vary depending upon our experiences in life. An idealistic teenager may have difficulty understanding the teachings of Jesus about judging others by remembering our own shortcomings. But as we grow older, we mellow with time and realize that we are far from perfect. Then it is that we can hear the

Master with new personal insight as he teaches, "Why do you see the speck that is in your brother's eye, but you do not notice the log that is in your own eye? Or how can you say to your brother, 'Let me take the speck out of your eye,' when there is the log in your own eye? You hypocrite, first take the log out of your own eye, and then you will see clearly to take the speck out of your brother's eye" (Matthew 7:3-5).

May these lessons in the faith help you and your loved ones to grow spiritually, to mature in the faith, and to have a better understanding of yourself as well as one another. May your eyes be opened to see our world with the eyes of faith, love and hope.

Kenneth A. Mortonson
Macomb, Illinois

Passages Of Scripture
For General Reflection

"At that time the disciples came to Jesus saying, 'Who is the greatest in the kingdom of heaven?' And calling to him a child, he put him in the midst of them, and said, 'Truly, I say to you, unless you turn and become like children, you will never enter the kingdom of heaven. Whoever humbles himself like this child, he is the greatest in the kingdom of heaven' " (Matthew 18:1-4).

"In that same hour he rejoiced in the Holy Spirit and said, 'I thank thee, Father, Lord of heaven and earth, that thou hast hidden these things from the wise and understanding and revealed them to babes; yea, Father, for such was thy gracious will' " (Luke 10:21).

"Come to him, to that living stone, rejected by men but in God's sight chosen and precious; and like living stones be yourselves built into a spiritual house, to be a holy priesthood, to offer spiritual sacrifices acceptable to God through Jesus Christ" (1 Peter 2:4, 5).

"For though by this time you ought to be teachers, you need some one to teach you again the first principles of God's word. You need milk, not solid food; for every one who lives on milk is unskilled in the word of righteousness, for he is a child. But solid food is for the mature, for those who have their faculties trained by practice to distinguish good from evil" (Hebrews 5:12-14).

Living In A Special Time

Purpose: To help children understand that every day is special.

Material: You will need some little special treat that can be shared with the children.

Lesson: Today we will be doing something very special.* We are going to baptize someone. This baby (or person) will not be baptized again, because we believe each person needs to be baptized only once. So something will happen here in our church today that will never happen again and that makes this a very special day. But you know what? Every day is a very special day for all of us. You will never be in church again on the last Sunday in July (or whatever Sunday it is) at your present age. Hopefully, you will be in church again next year on this Sunday, but by then you will be a year older.

So, the lesson I want you to learn today is very simple, yet very important. EACH DAY IS A SPECIAL DAY IN YOUR LIFE FOR THERE WILL NEVER BE ANOTHER DAY LIKE THIS. And I hope you will look for the special things in each day.

I tried to think of something I might give you to help make this a special day for you. I decided to share with you . . . *(Use whatever is appropriate: balloon, candy, homemade cookie, etc.)*. I hope you will enjoy this little treat and that it will help to make your day happy.

Possible Times To Use This Illustration In The Home:
- When your child is feeling unhappy because the weather is bad and he or she has to stay in the house.
- When your child has been to a special party.
- When a person has been baptized in your church.
- When you think the time is right for teaching your child to look for special things in each day.

*Adapting Note: This idea can be used in the home whenever you have a special occasion, like a birthday or the start of a school year, or some good news has come to the family. The point is to share with your child why today is special and then to go on from there to make the point that every day is special and we must look for the things and events that make it so.

Scriptural Background: "This is the day which the Lord has made; let us rejoice and be glad in it" (Psalm 118:24).

Beware Of Imitations

Purpose: To remind children not to accept imitations as something real.

Material: An artificial flower, an imitation gemstone; and perhaps a real flower and/or stone for comparison. A picture of Jesus, if available.

Lesson: This morning I want to show you something that I received in the mail (or wherever you might have obtained a cubic zirconia simulated diamond or artificial gemstone). What does it look like? ... (A diamond.) But it is not a diamond and I would be tricked by someone if it was sold to me as a diamond, for diamonds are very expensive, and this cost me nothing. (If you cannot find an imitation gemstone omit this part.) What is this? ... (A rose, or some other kind of flower.) But it is not a real flower, for it is made out of cloth and wire. It reminds me of a rose, but I cannot say that it is a rose for only God can create a real flower. *(Show a real flower, if you have one.)* Imitations help us to remember what something is like, but we must be careful not to think that the imitation is the real thing. Here is a picture of Jesus, but that is not Jesus. Its only purpose is to remind us of him.

One of our goals in life is to find the real life that God wants us to live. That requires hard work and a lot of learning. There are no shortcuts to the real thing. Anything less than the real life God desires for us is an imitation. So, remember that one of the reasons you come to church and study the Bible is because you want to find the real life God wants you to have. Your Sunday school teachers and everyone else who is with you each Sunday have that goal in mind for you, and you can help them help you by listening to them and doing what they teach you.

Possible Times To Use This Illustration In The Home:
- When a child does not want to go to Sunday school.
- When your child is spending too much time with computer games. (A real life is more than games.)
- When a child does not want to study.
- When a child is more interested in watching television than in learning new things.

Scriptural Background: "For the gate is narrow and the way is hard that leads to life, and those who find it are few" (Matthew 7:14).

Sending And Receiving

Purpose: To understand the importance of regular worship.

Material: A wireless microphone. If one is not available, a walkie-talkie will work. A battery, like the one used in your device.

Lesson: Today I want to show you something that we use every Sunday and that is very important to what we do.* This is called a wireless mike. When a person speaks into the little microphone here, the sound is sent out this wire and in a back room of the church there is a receiver that sends the sound through an amplifier and then out to the speakers so that people can hear what is said. I'd like you to try it. Tell me your name .... *(Let each child use the mike.)*

(Note: If you have to use the walkie-talkie, change the above. You might send one child to the back of the room to receive the sound in the second walkie-talkie set.)

Now, what makes this work is that there is a little battery inside. Without the power of a battery like this *(show)*, nothing would happen. But the battery itself needs to be recharged or replaced so that it can work. If it simply gives of its power, it will soon be no good.

One of the reasons why we say that people should come to church regularly is to receive new power for living. It is like getting our spiritual battery recharged or replaced so that we can take what we receive here and go out and share it with others.

Here we remember that God loves us and therefore, we can go out and love others. Here we learn about forgiveness so that we can go out and forgive others. Here we learn about all the good things God has done for us so we can go out and do good things for others. We receive so that we can give, like this wireless mike. Its purpose is to be a sender for the good of others. I hope you will learn to be like that, too.

Possible Times To Use This Illustration In The Home:
- When you have been to a worship service where a wireless microphone was used.
- Any time when you need to replace or recharge a battery.
- When your child questions why he or she has to go to church every Sunday.
- When you have been to a sports event where a referee has used a wireless mike.
- When your child is unwilling to share.

(Note: This concept of needing to be recharged can also be used to help a young child understand why getting a good night's rest is so important. Sleep is our way of recharging the body.)

*Adapting Note: If this lesson is used at home, you may use a flashlight. Simply show your child the battery that powers the unit.

Scriptural Background: "Come unto me, all who labor and are heavy-laden, and I will give you rest. Take my yoke upon you, and learn from me; . . . and you will find rest for your souls" (Matthew 11:28, 29).

Reading Faces

Purpose: To help children learn how to tell what another person might be feeling.

Material: Smiling face stickers, enough to hand out.

Lesson: One of the most important things you can do is to learn to read faces. Let me show you what I mean. When you see a face like this, what does it mean? . . . *(Look happy.)* And this? . . . *(Look sad.)* And this? . . .*(Look tired.)* The face of another person helps you to know how he or she is feeling and then you can respond to that message. If someone is sad and you are concerned about that person, you can try to make him feel better. Maybe your father and mother look tired at the end of a day and when you see their faces, you may decide it is not the time to ask them to come and play with you. Maybe you can even do something to help them with the housework so they won't be so tired. Reading faces helps us to consider how other people feel and then to respond accordingly. That is an important part of being a Christian.

Today I would like to share a smiling face sticker with you. You can use it to share happiness with someone else. I suggest you take this home and write a letter or draw a picture for a relative or your grandparents and send it to them with this sticker to make them happy. And remember to watch the other people in your home and watch your friends. Try to read their faces and respond to what you see. *(Be sure to give them a big smile as they leave.)*

Possible Times To Use This Illustration In The Home:
- When a child looks bored and needs to be encouraged to do something. Make a game of it. Suggest that the child watch some people outside or on television and see how many people he or she can tell are sad or happy just by the way they look and act. Later ask your child to share with you what was seen.
- When a child does not pay enough attention to the feelings of others.
- When your child has received a smiling face sticker from someone.

Scriptural Background: "When the days drew near for him to be received up, he set his face to go to Jerusalem" (Luke 9:51).

The Meaning Of Stewardship

Purpose: To think about the meaning of stewardship.

Material: A section of paper towel for each child.

Lesson: Today I want to use a paper towel to remind you of something very important. I want each one of you to have one of these. *(Give each child a section of paper towel.)*

Now, what could you do with this piece of paper towel? *(Wash windows, clean up a mess, help to keep your lap clean when you eat, shine your shoes, dry your hands after they have been washed, and so forth.)*

There are a lot of uses for a paper towel and most of them are to help us take care of things or of ourselves. The paper towel helps us to do what we call stewardship. Stewardship means taking care of what you have and making good use of it. It also means using what you have for the good of others as well as for your own good.

Each year, your parents and the other adults in the church are asked to think about the stewardship of their money. That means they need to think about how they will use their money for the good of your family and for the good of others. As part of this church, they also need to decide how much they will give to our church to help support our church family. It is a big decision for them to make. It is also very important to our church family.

Now, I want you to take this piece of paper towel home and try to be a good steward with it. See what good thing you can do with it there. Then remember to take good care of all that you have, for that is the meaning of stewardship.

Possible Times To Use This Illustration In The Home:
- When your child does not give enough thought to the proper use of what he or she has.
- When replacing a roll of paper towels at home.
- When you and your child see some other person misuse a possession.
- When your church is having its annual financial drive.

Scriptural Background: "So then, as we have opportunity, let us do good to all men, and especially to those who are of the household of faith" (Galatians 6:10).

What Do You Want From Christmas?

Purpose: To help children understand that there is more to Christmas than receiving gifts.

Material: Sheets of white paper (8½ x 11 inches) folded in quarters to form a card.

Lesson: I have a very important question to ask of you today. What do you want from Christmas? *(Wait for any answers.)* Remember, I asked what do you want FROM Christmas not what do you want for Christmas. There is a big difference. What we want from Christmas are the good things we can experience during this season and on Christmas Day. Let me tell you what I want from Christmas. I want Christmas to bring peace and happiness and love to all these people. I want Christmas to help us all know how beautiful life can be and I want Christmas to be a time when I can share my love of God and of life with others. I guess what I want from Christmas is to be able to share.

Now, I'd like you to experience this sharing in Christmas and so today I am going to give you a piece of plain paper which has been folded into a card. You can draw on it and color it or paste a Christmas picture on it; and inside you can write your own message to someone. Tell them that you hope their Christmas will be a happy time, or simply write that you want to share the Christmas Spirit with them. Then wish them a Merry Christmas. If you cannot write yet, I am sure your mother or father will help you.

Possible Times To Use This Illustration In The Home:
- During Advent, when you are addressing your Christmas cards.
- Before Christmas, when your child seems too concerned about what he or she will receive for Christmas.
- When you are trying to teach a small child about the meaning of Advent as a time to prepare for Christmas.

Scriptural Background: "And suddenly there was with the angels a multitude of the heavenly host praising God and saying, 'Glory to God in the highest, and on earth peace among men with whom he is pleased!' " (Luke 2:13, 14).

You Belong

Purpose: To think about what it means to be a part of a family.

Material: A picture of all your family together. Pieces of cardboard for making a picture frame. (Two pieces for each child.) A sample frame into which you have placed your picture.

Special Preparation: Make a sample to show. Two pieces of light cardboard can be used to make the frame. Decide on the size of the photo to be used and cut out a slightly smaller opening in the middle of one piece of cardboard. This piece can be colored or covered with a fabric. The second piece of cardboard will serve as the back.

Lesson: This morning I have a special picture I want to show you. Last summer, all my children were home at one time and all their children were with us, too. We had our picture taken and here you can see my wife and my children and my grandchildren. *(Use whatever family picture you have and tell the story about how the picture was taken.)*

Now, suppose something nice happens to one of the people in the picture. What effect do you think it would have on the other people in our family? ... (They would be happy.) And suppose something unpleasant happened to one of the people in this picture. What effect do you think that would have upon the other people in the family? . . . (They would be sad.)

You see, we sometimes forget that we belong to a family and what happens to us affects the other people in our family. Also, what we do within the family affects everyone else. For example: if you like to live in a nice, clean house, and you see a piece of paper on the floor, that you did not drop, what should you do? . . . (If you want a clean house, and you are part of the family, you should pick it up.)

Today I want to give you the material needed to make a picture frame like the one I have around my picture. You may need someone in your family to help you. I would like you to put a picture of your family in that frame so that it will remind you that you are a part of a special group of people. Remember, you belong to a group of people who love you and we want you to do your part to make your home a happy place to live.

Possible Times To Use This Illustration In The Home:
- When siblings are not getting along with each other.
- When looking at family photographs; or when you receive a family picture from a friend or relative.
- When you have been to a wedding or funeral. Comment on how important it is for the family to be together at such a time.

Scriptural Background: "When Jesus saw her weeping, and the Jews who came with her also weeping, he was deeply moved in spirit and troubled" (John 11:33).

Setting Things Right

Purpose: To help the children learn that they should be willing to aid people whom they can assist.

Material: No special material needed.

Lesson: When people say you have made a mistake, what do they mean by that? . . . (They think you did something wrong.) And what do you do when you really have made a mistake? . . . (You say you are sorry, and if you can, you try to set things right.)

Now what do you think you should do if you find that someone else has made a mistake? . . . *(Wait for possible answers. If there are no right answers, continue.)* Suppose you went home after church and found that someone had knocked over all the chairs around your kitchen table; what would you do? . . . (Set them up right so that you could sit on them to eat.) Suppose you saw someone sitting on a curb, holding his head and his head was bleeding; what would you do? . . . (Call for help so that they could set things right for that person.)

We call a person who helps others a good Samaritan. That is because Jesus told a story about a man who was from Samaria. That man found an injured person and he helped him, even though he did not know him. Whenever we see something that is not right or someone who needs help, we can often set things right by correcting their mistake or by offering to help the person in need, if we can. That is an important lesson for every Christian to remember.

Possible Times To Use This Illustration In The Home:
- When you and your child see someone helping another person.
- When a child refuses to clean up a mess because he or she did not cause it.
- When they make a mistake and a parent has to fix something.

Scriptural Background: "But a Samaritan, as he journeyed, came to where he was; and when he saw him, he had compassion, and went to him and bound up his wounds ..." (Luke 10:33, 34).

Summer Fun

Purpose: To motivate children to take some responsibility for filling up their free time with worthwhile activities.

Material: An envelope with a piece of paper folded and placed within it. (If you can afford it, place a stamp on the envelope.)

Lesson: Summer is a special time of the year. There are many things you can do, both inside and outside. Tell me, what do you like to do in the summer? . . . And what do you do when it is too hot to be outside, or when it rains? . . .

Today, I would like to suggest something that you might do when you have to be inside. Here is an envelope and a piece of paper that you can use to send a message to someone. If you cannot write, draw a picture; you might even do both. The important thing is that you want to let this other person know that you are thinking about him or her.

One of the ways we have of showing people that we care about them is to share something with them. In the summer, you can share with your friends as you play with them or do other things together. But it is also important to share your life with people who are away from you. Summer is a good time to think about how you can do this. Remembering others is an important part of life that all of us need to keep in mind.

Possible Times To Use This Illustration In The Home:
- When your child says there is nothing to do, or that he or she is bored.
- When a friend has moved away, or you have moved away.
- When you are trying to motivate a child to write to other relatives.

Scriptural Background: "A friend loves at all times, and a brother is born for adversity" (Proverbs 17:17).

The Shepherd's Staff

Purpose: To help children understand that Christmas is about caring for others.

Material: A homemade shepherd's staff. Candy canes to share.

Lesson: Do any of you know what this is called? ... This is a representation of a shepherd's staff. The shepherd had a stick like this that he used to help care for the sheep. With the hook, he could pull a little lamb out of the bushes or out of a hole in the ground, if it should happen to fall in. At night, when the sheep came back to the fold, to the place where they would sleep, the shepherd used the stick to block the doorway into the fold. In that way he could stop each sheep and look it over to see if it had any cuts that needed to be treated. Remembering this, we can say that the shepherd's staff is a symbol for caring, and Christmas is the time when we care for other people and give good gifts to them.

At Christmas time, we see a symbol of the shepherd's staff, but we call it by a different name. Does anyone know what that might be? ... It is the candy cane, which is a reminder of the shepherd's staff.

I have a candy cane for each one of you and I hope you will remember that part of the spirit of Christmas is to care for one another, not only today but all the time.

Possible Times To Use This Illustration In The Home:
- When a child is being selfish at Christmas time.
- When an older child is asked to help care for a younger sibling and is unwilling to do so.
- When you are talking to your child about the true meaning of Christmas.

Scriptural Background: "And when he comes home, he calls together his friends and his neighbors, saying to them, 'Rejoice with me, for I have found my sheep which was lost' " (Luke 15:6).

The New Year

Purpose: To use the beginning of a new year as a time to think about planning ahead.

Material: A calendar for each child. (You may be able to get a supply from your local bank or some other business.)

Lesson: This coming Tuesday (or whatever day it is) something special is going to happen. Who can tell me what it is? ... (The start of a new year.) We know it is a new year because the calendar tells us so.

The new year reminds us how important the calendar is to what we do. The calendar tells us when to celebrate our birthdays. It tells us when to go to school or come to church. It tells us what day of the week it is and what season of the year we are in. With that information, we can be prepared for what is to come. For example, if you want to send a birthday card to a special friend, you need to mark that date on a calendar as a reminder to get a card or get it mailed in time. So, the calendar reminds us that it is important to plan ahead for what is to come; and that is an important lesson for everyone.

Today, I have a calendar that you can take home for your own use. I suggest you mark the important dates on it and put it up in your room to remind you of the things you need to do. God has given us a brain so that we can plan ahead, and it is important to learn to do that. It helps us to be prepared for what is to come.

Possible Times To Use This Illustration In The Home:
- When a child has forgotten to do something important.
- When you are celebrating the start of a new year.
- At the start of a new year, take a calendar and help your child mark the important dates that need to be remembered.

Scriptural Background: "For which of you, desiring to build a tower, does not first sit down and count the cost, whether he has enough to complete it? Otherwise, when he has laid a foundation, and is not able to finish, all who see it begin to mock him, saying, 'This man began to build, and was not able to finish' " (Luke 14:28-30).

Flowers Follow Showers

Purpose: To think about using hard times for personal growth.

Material: Put some beautiful flowers in a paper sack. Bring them out when you talk about flowers.

Special Instructions: This illustration should be used in the spring when there have been a lot of rainy days.

Lesson: There is an old saying that reminds us of what has been happening this week. Let me see if any of you have heard it: "April showers bring ..." ("May flowers." *Share your flowers.*) We need to have rain in order for things to grow. Without the showers, there would be no flowers. This fact of life helps us to understand what often happens to us in life. We usually think of rainy days as dark and stormy. They may make it difficult for us to go some place or to do something special outside. Now, there may also be days in your life that may make you unhappy. Something happens, like a terrible storm, and you are frightened. We call these sad or frightening times hard times, but they can be important to us for they can help us to grow as we learn to handle them. When you are having a hard time, you need to ask yourself, "Why am I troubled and sad, and what can I do about it? Is there something I could have done differently that would have helped me avoid the problem? How can I change my attitude to help me get through this time?'' That is how you grow into a special, beautiful person. That is how you use the rainy times of life to blossom into that special person God created.

Possible Times To Use This Illustration In The Home:
- When your child is unhappy because a rainy day has caused a cancellation of a special event.
- In the spring, when the flowers are blooming in your garden.
- When a child is faced with any type of personal hardship.

Scriptural Background: ''More than that, we rejoice in our suffering, knowing that suffering produces endurance, and endurance produces character, and character produces hope, and hope does not disappoint us, because God's love has been poured into our hearts through the Holy Spirit which has been given to us'' (Romans 5:3-5).

Symbols Of Easter

Purpose: To understand why the date of Easter changes from year to year and to think about what that means for us.

Material: If available, a big picture of a full moon.

Lesson: Look at the people who are in church today. This must be a special day with so many people here. And so it is. This is Easter. Now, you may have noticed that Easter comes on a different day each year. That is because the date of Easter is set by the moon. Once it is spring, Easter is the first Sunday after the full moon. Last week spring started (or whenever it happened) and the first full moon in spring was on Wednesday (or whatever day). Today is the first Sunday after that full moon, and so it is Easter.

There are some special symbols in that fact. When we have a full moon, it is a bright light shining in the darkness. On that day, it is as bright as it can be at night. Now, we say that Jesus is the light of the world. John's gospel tells us that he is a light that shines in the darkness, and the darkness has not overcome it (Cf. John 1:5). Also, as we have more sunlight in the spring, we see life returning to the earth. Jesus is the true light of life that shines in the darkness and helps us to grow into the type of person God wants us to be. As we celebrate today, we must remember that, in Jesus, we are offered the way to a better life as we see that life in the light that shines from him.

Possible Times To Use This Illustration In The Home:
- When spring begins.
- When there is a full moon.
- When a child needs to be reminded of what Jesus offers us.

Scriptural Background: "In him was life, and the life was the light of men. The light shines in the darkness, and the darkness has not overcome it" (John 1:4, 5).

A Lesson From A Mirror

Purpose: To encourage children to be willing to accept help.

Material: A hand mirror.

Special Procedure: Before your time with the children, stick a piece of paper on your face.

Lesson: Most people use a mirror like this every day. They will look into it to see if their face is clean, or their hair looks all right or maybe to check out a sore on their face. You see, we cannot see our face like we can see our hands or feet.

Now, when you look at my face what do you see? ... Well, thank you for telling me. That looks silly; I better take it off. I saw it when I looked in the mirror, but then we were busy talking and I forgot what I saw. That was not a very smart thing for me to do.

So, sometimes we need other people to help us see things as they really are and to set them right. Sometimes we do something very silly and it helps when those who love us help us to see that thing in our life that needs to be changed for the better. I hope you will remember that when someone at home or school tries to help you. Thank you for helping me this morning.

Possible Times To Use This Illustration In The Home:
- When your child has accepted a type of behavior that is not pleasing to others in the family.
- When your child has been using a mirror to comb his or her hair, or some similar activity.
- When a child has been told something time and time again and fails to remember what to do.

Scriptural Background: "For if any one is a hearer of the word and not a doer, he is like a man who observes his natural face in a mirror; for he observes himself and goes away and at once forgets what he was like" (James 1:23, 24).

Riding A Train

Purpose: To help children understand why we need rules and regulations; and why they should be followed.

Material: A train ticket, if available; or a plastic credit card.

Lesson: Have any of you ever ridden on a train? . . . It is an interesting experience. Long ago, when people rode on the train, they bought a ticket from a person in the station, and when they got on the train, they gave the ticket to another person who was called the conductor. But this is not the case with many trains today. In Philadelphia, for example, the people boarding the train never see anyone who has anything to do with the operation of the train. At the train station, there is a machine that takes a five-dollar bill and returns five silver dollars. Then there is another machine into which the rider puts some of those silver dollars and out comes a plastic ticket that looks like a credit card. *(Show the card you have.)* The rider then uses the plastic ticket to unlock a gate that lets him or her into the station to get the train. When the train stops, the rider gets on the train and when it stops again at the desired place, the rider gets off and uses the plastic ticket to open a gate to get out of the station. During the ride, the people on board will hear a voice announcing the different stops, but outside of that, they have no contact with the people operating the train. There is no one there to check up on them, but if you want to ride the train, you have to follow the rules. You cannot get through the gates unless you do so.

That is a lesson that applies to life also. If you want to get the most out of life, you need to follow the rules. To have a friend, be a friend. Do unto others as you would have them do unto you. Love your neighbors. Part of growing up is learning about the rules of life that work; and Jesus is the best teacher in that regard. Jesus can open the gateway to true life.

Possible Times To Use This Illustration In The Home:
- When a child has ridden on such a train as described above.
- When a child fails to follow the rules.
- When a child tries to change the rules in a game.

Scriptural Background: "And as he was setting out on his journey, a man ran up and knelt before him, and asked him, 'Good Teacher, what must I do to inherit eternal life?' " (Mark 10:17).

Bubbles

Purpose: To learn that making certain choices in life can make a difference in what happens to us.

Material: Four small glasses. In one glass place a small amount of flour. In the next glass place a little baking soda. In the third glass pour some water, and in the final glass add a little clear vinegar. I suggest you identify each glass with a letter or notation on a piece of masking tape.

Lesson: Today I would like you to watch a simple experiment. First, notice what I have in these four glasses. In two glasses are white powders and in the other two glasses I have clear liquid. Now, I have marked each glass so that I will know what is in them. This is water and this is flour. Let's see what happens when I put the two together. If you wanted to make gravy, you would use a mixture like this. Now, let's see what happens when I put the other two together. This is baking soda and this is vinegar. When we want bubbles, we put these two together. *(Do so.)*

Now, what can we learn from this? Two things: If you want certain results, you need to put the proper things together. Also, if you want to produce something special, then you need to know what you can put together to produce that result. For example, if you want to know more about Jesus and God, then you need to put together spending time in Sunday school and at worship. Add to that reading your Bible and praying and you will find your life changing as the days go by as you learn and experience new things. Now, suppose you want to have friends. Living happily with other people requires certain things. You need to put together kindness and forgiveness and helping others. You can't be selfish all the time, if you want other people to like you. The Bible tells us that "a friend loved at all times . . ." (Proverbs 17:17), and a friend sticks closer than a brother or sister (Cf. Proverbs 18:24).

There is one other lesson here that we need to remember. In order to get the bubbles, I had to choose the right glasses. Part of growing up means learning to make the right choices. When you play a game with other people, you have to play according to the rules. If you do not, the other people will not want to play with you. One of the reasons we study the Bible is so that we can learn the rules about how God wants us to live. Since God created us, he knows what is the best way to live. When we do what God tells us to do, we get the best results out of living. I hope you will remember these things.

Possible Times To Use This Illustration In The Home:
- When you are working in the kitchen, especially if you are going to make gravy.
- When a child wants something special but is not willing to do what is needed to obtain that goal.
- When a child does something wrong and then is upset with the end result.

Scriptural Background: "An athlete is not crowned unless he competes according to the rules" (2 Timothy 2:5).

Freedom

Purpose: To help the children understand the nature of freedom.

Material: A long-sleeved shirt, or a regular straightjacket, if available. A bowl containing wrapped candy.

Lesson: Does anyone know what a straightjacket is? ... It is a special kind of jacket that has long arms, like this shirt, which can be tied behind a person so that person's arms are crossed in front of him like this. This morning I would like you to see what it would feel like to be in a straightjacket. Put your arms in front of yourself and take hold of your elbows, like this. Now, keep your hands there and do not let go of your elbows. Could you open a door? ... If your nose itched, could you scratch it? ... If I offered you a piece of wrapped candy, could you take it? ... You might pick it up with your teeth, but then how would you get it unwrapped?

How easy it is to lose some of our freedom. When we do lose it, then we begin to understand what a precious gift freedom is. Freedom is the ability to do what you think is right for you to do without restriction. I hope you boys and girls will always be thankful that you live in a country where people are free. Now, I have a bowl with some wrapped candy in it, and you are free to take one before you return to your seats.

Possible Times To Use This Illustration In The Home:
- When a child is studying past battles for freedom.
- When the news tells about people living under a dictator.
- When someone is unable to use one arm for a while.

Scriptural Background: "Jesus then said to the Jews who had believed in him, 'If you continue in my word, you are truly my disciples, and you will know the truth, and the truth will make you free' " (John 8:31, 32).

What Is Work?

Purpose: To help children understand the nature of work.

Material: No special material is needed.

Note: A good time to use this is Labor Day Weekend.

Lesson: Tomorrow is a special day in our country. Do you know what it is called? ... (Labor Day) Do you know why we have a Labor Day? ... It is to honor all the people who work. On your feet are shoes that I assume your parents bought for you at the store. Now the people in the store did not make those shoes; someone else did. That was their work; just as the people in the store work to help you buy things. Working is a very important part of our life together. It is what people do to accomplish something that needs to be done.

One of the difficult lessons of life that boys and girls have trouble learning is that there is joy in work when working accomplishes something. Coloring a picture with crayons is work, but it is also fun when you feel the pleasure of having a finished picture that is nicely colored and you can share that picture with someone. Learning to ride a bike is hard work; but once it is accomplished, it helps you travel fast and far. Cleaning up your room is hard work, but when it is done, it looks nice and usually you are able to find your things better when you need them. Every day we all have work that needs to be done, and we should be thankful that we have things to do and the strength and ability to do it. We should also be thankful for those who have done things for us.

Possible Times To Use This Illustration In The Home:
- When a child is asked to do some work around the house.
- When a child asks the parents why they have to go to work.
- When a child wonders why he or she has to go to school. (Part of getting an education is being prepared for one's life's work.)

Scriptural Background: "But we exhort you, ... to aspire to live quietly, to mind your own affairs, and to work with your hands, as we charged you; so that you may command the respect of outsiders, and be dependent on nobody" (1 Thessalonians 4:10-12).

What Do You Do When You Are Lost?

Purpose: To help children understand that they should seek help when they feel the need for such support.

Material: A large bandanna to use as a blindfold.

Lesson: I would like someone to volunteer to let me put a blindfold on you. *(Blindfold a child.)* Now, you cannot see, so I do not want you to move, because you could get hurt. Our blindfolded person knows where he (or she) is, but he cannot get back to the place where he was seated. It is up to one of you to help him. What could you do? . . . Take his hand and lead him back. Tell him how to walk and when to turn. That would take longer, but it could be done. And if his parents would help talk him back at the other end, that would help, too. *(Take off the blindfold.)*

There is an important lesson for us here. Our blindfolded friend is like someone who is lost, and that person could be you. Being lost means you cannot get back to where you want to be. In that condition, what do you need? . . . You need someone to guide you or to tell you what to do. Now, that person could mislead you. So, the one you receive help from must be someone you can trust. If the time ever comes that you feel lost, turn to someone you trust for help. You should be able to find such a person at home or in your church home or in a teacher at school.

Possible Times To Use This Illustration In The Home:
- When a child has been lost while the family is shopping.
- When a game has been played that used a blindfold, like pin the tail on the donkey.
- After seeing a movie or hearing a story about someone who was lost.

Scriptural Background: "For the Son of man came to seek and to save the lost" (Luke 19:10).

The Lesson Of "O"

Purpose: To remind children that the good life requires the presence of God; and with God, we will love one another.

Material: You will need several pieces of large paper or poster board. On one, make a large circle. On the front of another, print the word "GOD." On the back, print "GOOD." You will also need a poster with the letter "I" on it. And on another, print "LIVE" on one side and "LOVE" on the other side. You will also need enough donut holes to share.

Lesson: Today I would like you to do a few things with the figure "O." *(The letter "O" can be formed with your fingers.)* This shape can represent several things. Can you tell me what they are? . . . (The letter O and zero. It is also called a circle.) Now, let's see what happens to the word GOOD *(Show that side of poster.)* if you take "GOD" out of it. *(Turn the poster over.)* What is left? . . . (Zero; or nothing.) Without God we cannot know what is good. Without God, we have nothing. *(Show the poster that has the circle on it.)*

Now, let's call our figure a circle. When we have a circle, it surrounds everything that is inside the circle. *(You may let the children form a circle around you.)* The circle reminds us that we need to include other people in our lives. When we like someone, sometimes we put our arms around him or her.

We need to reach out to people and let them be a part of our lives.

Again, we have two words that help us to remember this. First, what does this letter ("I") stand for? It represents a person whom we call "I." That person can live *(Show L-I-V-E on the poster board.)*, but to have the full life God wants us to have, we need to let others live with us. We need that circle we just talked about. Let's see what happens if we replace the "I" with the circle "O." What do we have now? (LOVE) Jesus said, we are to love one another to show that we are his followers (Cf. John 13:34).

The donut is shaped like an "O," but we have been thinking about what is included in the "O," so instead of a donut, I have a donut hole for each one of you.

Possible Times To Use This Illustration In The Home:
- When your child has excluded a friend from his or her play time.
- When a child does not want to take part in a group activity.
- When you have shared a donut or donut hole with your child.

Scriptural Background: "I am the vine, you are the branches. He who abides in me, and I in him, he it is that bears much fruit, for apart from me you can do nothing" (John 15:5).

Don't Worry

Purpose: To help children exert some personal effort when faced with a problem.

Material: An egg. If available, a toy or live chick.

Lesson: Today I want you to look at something that I am sure you have seen before. *(Show them an egg.)* What comes out of this egg? ... If it is allowed to hatch, in a normal way, a chick will come out of it. And the way it comes out is to break through the shell from the inside, when the time is right. Now, if you were to see the chick trying to break out of the shell and you said, "Maybe that baby chicken will not get out. I will help him," that would be the wrong thing to do, for the work of getting out of the shell helps to strengthen the little chick.

Sometimes, you may have trouble with something, and you worry about doing it right, and your first thought is to ask for help. Because you are worried and you think you may not do it right, you are unwilling to try. And sometimes, the person whom you ask to help will not help you right away. When people care about you, they may want you to keep on trying because that is the best thing for you. So, when you have a problem, don't worry. Remember the egg and do all you can to take care of your problem; and then, when you have done all you can, you can ask for help if it is still needed.

Possible Times To Use This Illustration In The Home:
- When your child has a problem and is unwilling to even try to work at the solution.
- When a child says something is too hard to do.
- When you have seen a live baby chick.

Scriptural Background: "Therefore, my beloved, as you have always obeyed, so now, not only as in my presence but much more in my absence, work out your own salvation with fear and trembling; for God is at work in you, both to will and to work for his good pleasure" (Philippians 2:12, 13).

The Importance Of Giving Thanks

Purpose: To help children to remember that part of being human means giving thanks.

Material: A batch of homemade cookies (or some other homemade treat) to share.

Lesson: Do any of you have a dog at home? ... Do you do anything special when you feed your dog? ... In our house, we have the dog do a trick, like sitting up, before she is fed. And you know what she does when we put the food down? She eats it right away. And you know what else? She never says, "Thank you."

Now, of course, I don't expect her to say thank you, because she is a dog. But I do expect people, like you, who can talk to say thank you when someone gives you something or does something nice for you. When you say thank you to someone you are showing them that you like what they have done for you, that you are happy to have received their special gift. And when you are happy with what has been done for you, then the person doing it shares your happiness; and that is good. Showing appreciation is a very special way of sharing with one another.

Yesterday I made some cookies and I'd like to share them with you this morning. You may take one as you return to your seats. *(If they all say, "Thank You," you can comment on the fact that they are quick learners.)*

Possible Times To Use This Illustration In The Home:
- When your child fails to show appreciation for what others do for him or her.
- When you want to explain to your child why you say grace at meals.
- When you want to encourage your child to say grace.

Scriptural Background: "Rejoice always, pray constantly, giving thanks in all circumstances; for this is the will of God in Christ Jesus for you" (1 Thessalonians 5:16-18).

Why Do We Want To Learn?

Purpose: To help children understand the importance of learning new things.

Material: You will need one large jar and two smaller jars. In one small jar, using food coloring, place yellow water. In the other small jar, place blue water.

Lesson: How many of you boys and girls are going or plan to go to school? . . . Why do people go to school? . . . Learning new things is very important for everybody, even for adults. We never outgrow our need to learn. The reason for this is that the new things we learn change us; and the more we know, the more we can do; and life will be fuller.

Let me illustrate what I mean. When people are born, they don't know very much. But as they grow and learn, new things are added to their life. *(Pour the blue water into the large jar.)* Then, as they grow older, they learn different things, as represented by this yellow water. Now, do you know what will happen when I add these two colors together? . . . If you have been to school you probably know that yellow and blue make green. Let's see if it works. . . . We now have a new color, green. Green is a very special color. It is the color of things that are growing. It tells us that life is present and active in many plants. It is a good color to remind us that we all need to keep on learning and growing. We all need to be adding new things to our store of knowledge. As we do so, year after year, life will change and be better. That is why we should never stop learning new things.

Possible Times To Use This Illustration In The Home:
- When a child does not want to go to school, or take time to read.
- When you, as a parent, are learning new things.
- When using food coloring in the kitchen.

Scriptural Background: "That men may know wisdom and instruction, understand words of insight, . . . the wise man also may hear and increase in learning, and the man of understanding acquire skill" (Proverbs 1:2, 5).

Prayer

Purpose: To help children understand the nature of prayer.

Material: If you feel it is safe to do so, you might have a prayer written on a piece of paper and burn it on a metal tray.

Lesson: Today I want to talk to you about something we do together each Sunday and which I assume you have done at home. We call it "praying." You may use prayers in your family when you sit down to have a meal or when you are getting ready to go to sleep. These are special times for prayers, but I hope you know that you can pray anytime, anywhere.

Long ago people used altars and smoke and fire to help them when they prayed. Back then, a person might write a prayer on a piece of paper and then set the paper on fire on an altar, and as the smoke rose the one praying felt that what was desired in prayer was being carried to the gods in the heavens.

Today, however, because of Jesus, we believe that we do not need such things to help us pray. All we have to do is to talk to God as we would talk to a friend or to our parents. You see, when Jesus taught his disciples to pray, he told them to begin by saying, "**Our Father**, who art in heaven ..." (Matthew 6:9).

Prayer is very important to your life as a Christian, for it is one way that you can bring God into your life, just as you let a friend be a part of your life when you talk to that person. Remember, God is everywhere so to talk to him all you need to do is to think the thoughts that you want to share with him and they shall be shared. I hope you boys and girls will take time, every day, to let your thoughts go to God in prayer.

Possible Times To Use This Illustration In The Home:
- When on a picnic or camping and you are sitting around a campfire.
- When at home watching the fire in a fireplace.
- When you are teaching your child to say grace at the table or to say a prayer at bedtime.

Scriptural Background: "Let the words of my mouth and the meditation of my heart be acceptable in thy sight, O Lord, my rock and my redeemer" (Psalm 19:14).

The Door

Purpose: To help children see the importance of being willing to spend time learning about Jesus.

Material: No special material is needed.

Lesson: This morning, as always, I came into the sanctuary by way of a door. You also came into the church through a doorway. A door is a very interesting thing. I remember learning a little song in Sunday school, a long time ago, that began:

"One door and only one and yet its sides are two.

Inside and outside, on which side are you?"

The door is a symbol for making a decision. You may choose to stay on one side; or you may decide to open the door and go through it to the other side. But you cannot be on both sides at the same time.

We find this happening to us every day. We have to make a decision about where we want to be. For example, when the hour comes for the time of worship on Sunday morning and you have not passed through a door into a place of worship, then you have decided not to be in church that day, which means you decided to do something else.

Jesus referred to himself as a door. In John 10:9, we hear him say, "I am the door; if anyone enters by me, he will be saved, and will go in and out and find pasture." He used that illustration as he was talking about being the Good Shepherd.

What he meant was that he was the way through which we can find what we really need for the living of life. But we have to decide to spend time with him if we are to learn from him.

"One door and only one and yet its sides are two.
Inside and outside, on which side are you?"

Possible Times To Use This Illustration In The Home:
- When the family is building a house. The location of the door frames illustrates the need for a door.
- When you are unlocking a door, so that you may leave or someone may enter the house.
- When you are decorating a door for the holidays.

Scriptural Background: "For he that is not against us is for us" (Mark 9:40).

The Silent Language

Purpose: To help children see things in a new way.

Material: You will need a small pane of glass.

Lesson: What do you see in my hand? . . . Your first answer might be simply, "A piece of glass." But look again and think about how you might use this piece of glass. What do you see? . . . If you were a homeowner, you might see a pane of glass for a broken window. If you have fish in the house, this might be a cover for a fish bowl, to keep the goldfish in and the cat out. If you like to garden, you might see this as a protection for a table top upon which a flower pot might be placed. If you were an artist, this could be a surface upon which to mix some colors if you were painting with oil paint. This piece of glass is a very simple object and yet it can have different meanings to just as many different people.

I find that very interesting. We can learn something about people just by seeing how they make use of what is around them. And how we use the things that we have tells other people something about us. Now, as Christians, we want people to see that we are followers of Jesus, and that means using what we have for the good of others as well as for ourselves. That is part of what we mean by stewardship.

We come to church to try to see things in a new way, to see things as God sees them. And the closer we come to seeing life as God wants us to see it, the closer we come to finding true life. So, keep your eyes and ears and heart and mind open here. What you find in church may surprise you; and it may help you see life in a different way. And that may change the way you use all the things you will have in life.

Possible Times To Use This Illustration In The Home:
- When you need to replace a broken window.
- When your child is working with paints.
- When your child rebels against going to church.

Scriptural Background: "For my thoughts are not your thoughts, neither are your ways my ways, says the Lord" (Isaiah 55:8).

Standing On Two Feet

Purpose: To help children understand why religious education is essential to true life.

Material: No special material is needed.

Lesson: This morning, I would like each one of you to stand up. Now, stand on just one foot and as soon as you lose your balance and have to touch the floor with the other foot, sit down. Some people find that they can stand on one foot for a long time, but such people usually have to concentrate on what they are doing to maintain their balance.

Now, everybody stand on two feet again. Which way is easier? ... It is much easier for us to stand or move about when we use both feet. Our feet give us a special stability in life when we use them properly.

This is also true in regard to the things we learn in life. All of you are, or will be, expected to go to school during the week. There are basic things that you must learn to be able to function properly in life as you grow up. But that education is just part of what you need. It is like standing on one foot.

In the church, we believe that in order to be a complete person you also need to learn the things that are offered to you on Sunday in the church school program. This is like the second foot that enables you to stand or move about through life.

So, I hope you will remember how important it is to get a complete education. Your Sunday education is just as important as your weekday education. I hope you will pay attention both here and at school so that you can learn all the important things you need for life.

Possible Times To Use This Illustration In The Home:
- At the start of a new school year.
- When you have been to a circus and watched someone on a high wire.
- When a child is unwilling to learn new things.

Scriptural Background: "The fool says in his heart, 'There is no God.' They are corrupt, they do abominable deeds, there is none that does good" (Psalm 14:1).

Changing Nature

Purpose: To show that the type of world we live in affects us.

Material: The wildflower, Queen Anne's Lace. Red food dye.

Special Procedure: Cut two flowers from the wildflower known as Queen Anne's Lace. Place one cut stem in water colored with red food dye. Let it remain in the water until the flower is colored. (If Queen Anne's Lace is not available, you might try another white flower to see if it will work also.)

Lesson: This morning I would like you to look at something that we can see everywhere at this time of the year. Does anyone know what this flower is called? . . . (Queen Anne's Lace.) Notice how nice and white it is. Now, let me show you a different Queen Anne's Lace. This one is colored red. Let me tell you how I did this. After I cut off the flower and took it home, I placed it in a glass of water that I colored by adding red food dye. Then I just waited and in a day or so, the flower took on the color of its new surroundings.

The lesson from this is simple. The conditions under which we live have an effect upon us. If the people in your house are always fighting with one another that will make you feel unhappy inside and it will show in the way you look and act. The things you watch on television can affect how you feel about what is important in life and that can affect what you do. The type of friends you have can also affect the way you behave. We all need to be careful about the conditions that surround us as we live each day, for they can influence how we feel inside. And how we feel inside can change how we act toward other people. Now, I hope your time in church will help you to know that you are loved by God and by the members of your church family. Knowing that, I hope it will make you happy and that you will be more loving to others.

Possible Times To Use This Illustration In The Home:
- In the spring, when the weeds appear.
- When a child is careless about the condition of the interior of your house.
- At Easter, when you are coloring eggs.

Scriptural Background: "And so, from the day we heard of it, we have not ceased to pray for you, asking that you may be filled with the knowledge of his will in all spiritual wisdom and understanding, to lead a life worthy of the Lord, fully pleasing to him, bearing fruit in every good work and increasing in the knowledge of God" (Colossians 1:9, 10).

The Strength Of Togetherness

Purpose: To help children understand the importance of working together.

Material: A piece of notebook paper for each child. A piece of plywood.

Lesson: This morning, I would like to do a little experiment with you. I would like each one of you to take a piece of paper and see if you can tear it in half. Now, let me have the two pieces of paper and put them all together. Can anyone tear them all in half? ... *(Repeat until the many layers of paper cannot be torn.)*

Soon we get to the place where all the paper together is too strong and no one can tear it. Plywood is another example of this truth. This is a piece of plywood and as you can see, it has three layers, which make it stronger than each layer alone.

This is an important lesson for life. People together can do many things that people alone could not do. But for that to happen, people need to be close to one another and to share life together if they are to strengthen each other. And the more people who are willing to work together, the better.

This applies to the home as well as to the church. So, once again, we see how important you are, for you are part of our togetherness. As you help others, you strengthen your church and your home. The opposite is also true. When you are unwilling to cooperate with others, the unity of that special group to which you belong is broken.

Possible Times To Use This Illustration In The Home:
- When your child is unwilling to cooperate with other people in the family.
- When your child needs to be encouraged to be a part of a team.
- When your child is using paper, for whatever reason.

Scriptural Background: "For just as the body is one and has many members, and all the members of the body, though many, are one body, so it is with Christ" (1 Corinthians 12:12).

What Is A Lie?

Purpose: To help children understand why lying is wrong.

Material: No special material is needed.

Lesson: What is a lie? ... A lie is something that is stated as being true when it is not true. Why do you think it is wrong to tell a lie? ... Because it can hurt people.

Let me show you what I mean. If I invited you to a party and told you that it would be held tomorrow at 3:00 p.m. when I knew it was going to be held this afternoon at 3:00 p.m., how would you feel if you came to my house tomorrow and no one was home? ...

Suppose you are playing baseball and you hit the ball and break a window and the owner of the house comes out and asks, "Who broke my window?" What happens if no one tells the truth? ... The owner has to buy a new window and he is hurt because he does not know the truth. He has to pay to fix something that he did not break.

You see, it is very important for people to have the truth in life if they are to avoid being hurt by something that was not their fault. Sometimes telling the truth may cause you to have to face the consequences of what you did and that may hurt you; but if you lie to save yourself some pain, you will probably hurt someone else. If we love one another we cannot do that.

Possible Times To Use This Illustration In The Home:
- When your child has told a lie.
- When someone in the family has been hurt by someone else telling a lie.
- When your child has failed to take responsibility for something that he or she has broken.

Scriptural Background: "Love does no wrong to a neighbor; therefore love is the fulfilling of the law" (Romans 13:10).

Being At Peace With One Another

Purpose: To encourage children to do their part in building friendships or being at peace with someone else.

Material: Two jars and two small candles. Place one candle in a jar. Fasten the other candle to a piece of wood — in the center — so that it can float and stand upright, in the jar. (Experiment at home.) You will also need a way to add water to both jars. A baster will work. Matches to light the candles.

Lesson: I have a special situation here in these two jars that I want you to look at this morning. In each jar is a candle that is burning. Now, what do you think will happen if I add water to each jar? Let's see.

Well, that one went out because fire and water cannot exist together in the same place. But this one is still burning, for there is something else in this jar. The candle is on a piece of wood and the wood floats on the water and that keeps the water away from the fire. So both can exist together in the jar.

This reminds us of something we all need to remember as we live with other people. There are times when we have to add something special to prevent a problem. That something special that we can add is to be a peacemaker. That means, we will do what we can to keep a friend.

What do you do if someone hits you? ... Hitting back is one thing you can do; or you can be a peacemaker and not hit back. You can do a lot of things to keep a friend as a friend. You can do it because you have something special that we call love. And when we love one another then we will find a way to get along and not hurt each other. I hope you will keep this in mind as you live and play with others.

Possible Times To Use This Illustration In The Home:
- When a child complains about not having friends.
- When your children have been fighting with one another.
- When someone has been picking on your child.

Scriptural Background: "But I say to you, 'Do not resist one who is evil. But if any one strikes you on the right cheek, turn to him the other also' " (Matthew 5:39).

Hands

Purpose: To share with the children the wonder of our hands and to encourage them to use their hands for good.

Material: No special material is needed.

Lesson: This morning I want you to think for a few moments about something you all have. In fact you have two of them. They are out in the open where everyone can see them. You used them this morning to get dressed and to eat your breakfast and to brush your teeth. Does anyone know what I am thinking about? ... What is it? (HANDS!)

We are told that the movement of the hand is governed by 30 different joints and more than 50 muscles. Every day we use these hands to perform nearly 1,000 different functions. Our hands are very special because of the way they work and they are perfectly coordinated with the eye and mind. Our hands are indeed a most wonderful part of our body. We should thank God, our Creator, for them.

It is important for you to remember that you can use your hands in so many ways, for good or bad. You can be greedy with your hands and hold on to things, or you can share with your hands. You can use your hand to hurt someone or you can use your hand to be a friend.

So, today, I want you to remember how important your hands are and to try to use your hands for good things so that by your hands the people around you will know what a good person you are.

Now, as you go back to your places, I would like each one of you to shake hands with the other boys and girls and with me.

Possible Times To Use This Illustration In The Home:
- When your child has been using his or her hands in a destructive way.
- When someone in the family has hurt a hand and cannot use it for a while.
- When your child needs to be encouraged to practice a musical instrument.

Scriptural Background: "So they remained for a long time, speaking boldly for the Lord, who bore witness to the word of his grace, granting signs and wonders to be done by their hands" (Acts 14:3).

The Control Center

Purpose: To stress the importance of learning to listen and to be receptive to what others say.

Material: A remote control from a television set.

Lesson: This morning I have an interesting little gadget that I think some of you have probably seen or used. Do you know what this is? ... It is called a remote control. And do you know what it is used for? ... With a remote control, you can make things happen by just pushing a button.

So, let's see what happens when I push the "on" button. Nothing happened. Why? ... Because there has to be something around that can be turned on or off by this remote control. I can push this button and it will send out a signal, but nothing happens because there is no television set here to receive that signal.

The lesson of this is simple. What is sent must be received, or nothing will happen. And the lesson applies to many things. God sent his love to us in Jesus, but if we do not receive it, nothing happens. Your parents send you a message of what they want you to do, but if you do not accept what they say, or if you fail to remember what they said, nothing will happen in the way your parents want it to happen. If your friend does not really listen to you when you talk, nothing will change because of what you said.

So we all need to listen when people speak to us, and we want others to listen to us when we speak. This is an essential part of learning to get along with other people. It is also an important lesson for your parents as well as for you.

Possible Times To Use This Illustration In The Home:
- When your child is having trouble listening to his parents or teachers.
- When your child seems to have a closed mind in church.
- When you have been using the remote control while watching television.

Scriptural Background: "And I heard the voice of the Lord saying, 'Whom shall I send, and who will go for us?' Then I said, 'Here I am! Send me' " (Isaiah 6:8).

We All Need Help

Purpose: To encourage children to seek help when they need it.

Material: A hearing aid. A pair of glasses. (Borrow them, if you do not have either of these.)

Special Procedure: If possible, be seated when you are talking to the children.

Lesson: This morning I have something I want to show you that you may not have seen before. Does anyone know what this is? ... (A hearing aid.) And what is it used for? ... (To help a person hear better.) Some people are not able to hear as well as you do so they have to wear a hearing aid that magnifies the sound so that they can hear better. Isn't that wonderful? It's just like these glasses. Some people wear glasses so that they can see better.

Now, what would you think of a person who needed a hearing aid or glasses and could afford to buy them, but did not? ... That's not very smart, is it? And what would you think about a boy or girl who wants to learn how to ride a bike, but will not let anyone help? ... That's not very smart, either.

The point I want you to remember is that there are times when we all need help and wise is the person who will ask for help when it is needed.

Now, will someone please help me get up? Thank you.

Possible Times To Use This Illustration In The Home:
- When your child needs help but is unwilling to accept it.
- When someone in the family needs new glasses, or a grandparent needs a hearing aid.
- When you want to encourage your child to help around the house.

Scriptural Background: "He who has ears to hear, let him hear" (Matthew 11:15).

Happy New Year Noises

Purpose: To think about what influences life.

Material: Noisemakers

Lesson: Did any of you stay up last night (or whenever New Year's Eve was) until midnight? . . . Many people do this. They stay up until that time so that they can welcome in the new year. And very often people welcome in the new year with noisemakers like these. *(Share whatever noisemakers you can find. Let them make noise together.)* This is a very old custom. It goes back to the time when people thought that there were bad spirits about and these bad spirits could cause them all kinds of trouble. People also thought that by making a lot of noise, they could scare the bad spirits away and the bad spirits would not enter the new year with them. It was a way of asking for good things to happen to them in the coming year. Now, it may be fun to make a lot of noise on New Year's Eve, but we believe that the blessings of life come to us, not by keeping bad spirits away, but by living with God. We believe that all things work together for good to those who love God (Cf. Romans 8:28). So the important thing for us to remember in the New Year is to love God and follow his teachings and to ask him to be with us every day. Let's do that together in a prayer. *(Use your own prayer.)*

Possible Times To Use This Illustration In The Home:
- When a child blames other people or things for his or her misfortune.
- When a child has been allowed to stay up until midnight on New Year's Eve.
- When a young child is afraid that some kind of monster is in the shadows or in the closet.

Scriptural Background: "What then shall we say to this? If God is for us, who is against us? He who did not spare his own Son but gave him up for us all, will he not also give us all things with him?" (Romans 8:31, 32).

A Lesson From A Shell

Purpose: To remind the children of the importance of each day and to make the most of each day.

Material: Seashells or pictures of seashells. (If you have a large quantity of seashells, you may want to share one with each child.)

Lesson: Have any of you ever been to Florida? One of the things people like to do in Florida is to walk the beach and look for shells. There are all kinds of shells to be found every day on the beaches, and shells come in all kinds of shapes. *(Show actual shells or pictures of shells.)*

The shell is the protective covering on different kinds of creatures who live in the sea. Each day new shells are washed up on the beaches of the oceans. The little creature who lived in the shell is gone, but the shell remains.

We do not live in shells, but there is a lesson for us here in the shell. Each day, we leave something of our self behind, for good or bad. When we are kind to others and try to make other people happy, we leave a good memory behind that adds beauty to life. Once the day is over, we cannot change that memory. It is like the shell: what we have done is set. Remember, with each new day, you have a new chance to do good things that will produce good memories.

(If you have a number of shells, you might give each child one as a reminder of your time together.)

Possible Times To Use This Illustration In The Home:
- When you are on a vacation that enables you to find seashells.
- When your child has had a day of bad behavior and does not seem to be concerned about it.
- It can also be used when he or she has had an especially good day.

Scriptural Background: "The memory of the righteous is a blessing, but the name of the wicked will rot" (Proverbs 10:7).

Surprise!

Purpose: Helping children to find joy in each day.

Material: Prepare a little surprise package for each child. Your surprise can be anything from a picture to color, to a treat, to a sticker, to whatever is available to you in an amount to cover the number of children present.

Lesson: Have you ever had a nice surprise? ... What is a nice surprise? ... (Something nice happens to you that you did not expect to happen.) We have surprises happening to us every day. When someone gives you a smile and says hello to you, that is a nice surprise. Do you know what you will have for dinner today? ... Maybe it will be a nice surprise. When you watch television, you do not know what will happen in the story you are watching. ... That is a surprise. Each day is filled with nice surprises and, therefore, we should look forward to each day and be happy with all the nice, new things that happen to us.

You see, each day is special. Long ago a person who had faith in God discovered that each day was filled with many wonders and surprises and he wrote: "This is the day which the Lord has made; let us rejoice and be glad in it" (Psalm 118:24).

Now, I have a surprise for each one of you, but I want you to wait until you get home to open it. And have a nice, surprise-filled day.

87

Possible Times To Use This Illustration In The Home:
- After a birthday party.
- When your child seems bored with life.
- Whenever something surprising has happened in the family.

Scriptural Background: "I will call to mind the deeds of the Lord; yea, I will remember thy wonders of old" (Psalm 77:11).

What Day Is This?

Purpose: To help children learn what to do when they make a mistake.

Material: No special material is needed.

Special Procedure: This object lesson should be used at a time when the children will know that it is not the date you say, like in winter, or at the start of the new year.

Lesson: Good morning. Today is the third of July. Right? ... It's not July third? ... Well, what am I going to do? ... You think I made a mistake? ... Maybe I should just go home? ... You must think I am dumb since I don't know what day it is.

Sometimes boys and girls want to run and hide when they say or do something wrong, but that doesn't solve the problem. What else can I do? ... I could refuse to admit that I was wrong and say you are wrong if you think this is not July third. But that would just be stubbornness on my part and nothing would get corrected that way.

What else can I do? ... I can ask you to help me and tell me what day this is. That is a good thing to do when you discover you made a mistake. We all make mistakes and need to learn from others. All of us like to be happy in life, and one of the best ways to find happiness is to learn what to do when you make a mistake. You can always ask for help.

Now, what day is this? ... Right. Thank you for setting me straight.

Possible Times To Use This Illustration In The Home:
- When your child needs help in learning how to handle making a mistake.
- When your child needs to be encouraged to ask for help when help is needed.
- When your child is too stubborn.

Scriptural Background: "My brethren, if any one among you wanders from the truth and some one brings him back, let him know that whoever brings back a sinner from the error of his way will save his soul from death and will cover a multitude of sins" (James 5:19, 20).

Nuts*

Purpose: To help children to persevere when faced with a problem.

Material: A nut or two. A treat, to share, made with nuts.

Lesson: This morning I want to show you something that we can find on certain trees at this time of the year. They are called nuts. A nut is an interesting thing. It is a seed with a hard shell and what is inside the shell is usually good to eat.

The nut is a symbol of something we face all the time in life. We sometimes call a difficult person a "nut" because the reason for his or her behavior is hidden from us. Or we say that a problem is a hard nut to crack. The nut is a reminder that there are a lot of good things in life that we have to work at to get.

For example, learning how to read is a wonderful thing to be able to do, but you have to work at it in order to learn. Learning to play a musical instrument is very enjoyable, but you have to practice to learn to play.

The important thing is to remember that what you are seeking on the other side of that shell requires work on your part and you must be willing to do it to get the fruit of your labors.

Now I'd like to share the fruit of my labors by giving you a homemade cookie this morning; and, of course, the cookie has nuts in it.

Possible Times To Use This Illustration In The Home:
- In the fall, when you have been gathering nuts.
- When you have prepared something to eat that contains nuts.
- When your child needs encouragement to continue doing anything that is hard to do.

Scriptural Background: "Brethren, do not be weary in well-doing" (2 Thessalonians 3:13).

*For use in the fall.

The Easter Lily

Purpose: To help children understand the meaning of Easter.

Material: An egg. An Easter lily.

Lesson: There are many symbols around us in the church today. Do you know what a symbol is? . . . It is something that
reminds us of something else. The decorated evergreen trees
remind us of Christmas and the lilies remind us of Easter.

The important part of a symbol is to remember what it
stands for. The Easter egg is a symbol of Easter because, at
the right time, an egg can break open and we have new life
in the chick that is born.

Let's look at the Easter lily and see what symbols are here.
The flower is like a trumpet that proclaims this great day. White
is the color of maximum light and reminds us of Jesus, who
said, "I am the light of the world" (John 8:12). Inside the flower we see little specks of gold. Jesus said that He came so that
we might have abundant life (Cf. John 10:10). Gold is a symbol of richness and abundance.

See this little thing, in the center of the flower, which has
three bumps on it? It is one thing but it has three parts. It reminds us that we know God in three ways as Father, Son and
Holy Spirit.

Green is the color of things growing. The green leaves remind us that we are to grow into true life with Jesus, for the Son came to help us see the true nature of God.

The lily grows from a bulb, which is like a tomb, and bursts forth with new life at Easter. So the lily is a good symbol to help us to remember what we celebrate today. In Jesus we have a new, rich, beautiful life; we have life as God wants it to be.

Possible Times To Use This Illustration In The Home:
- When an Easter lily is brought into the house.
- When you are preparing for Easter.
- When you are planting bulbs.

Scriptural Background: "The thief comes only to steal and kill and destroy; I came that they might have life, and have it abundantly" (John 10:10).

A Lesson From A Broken Arm

Purpose: To help children understand the need to take time to consider important things.

Material: Make a sling that you can put on to hold your arm.

Lesson: This is what is known as a sling. Does anyone know what it is used for? ... Right. To hold your arm still after you have injured it. Have any of you ever had a broken arm? ... When that happens, you have to keep your arm still for a long time. Then, when you can finally use your arm again, you find it is rather weak. Because the muscles have not been used regularly, they get weak and you have to start exercising that arm to make it strong.

This reminds us of an important lesson in life. That which you do not use, you tend to lose. If you sit at home all day — day after day — watching television, you could get weak. If you do not try to learn new things, you soon have difficulty remembering things. Great athletes and musicians practice all the time so that they can keep their skills. If you do not spend time with a friend, soon that person is no longer your friend.

The same thing applies to our knowledge of God. When people fail to spend time thinking about God and learning about God, soon God is not important to them and they lose that sense of fellowship with him. So, if you don't want to lose your ability to walk or play an instrument or read or have a friend or know God, then be sure to spend time doing what is important to you and don't let just one thing take up all your time.

Possible Times To Use This Illustration In The Home:
- When someone breaks an arm or leg.
- When your child is spending too much time on one thing.
- When your child needs to be encouraged to try doing something new.

Scriptural Background: "Seek the Lord while he may be found, call upon him while he is near" (Isaiah 55:6).

What Do You Do With Dust?

Purpose: To help children remember that we are all responsible for the kind of world we live in.

Material: A dust-laden object. A dust rag. A half dozen or so small pieces of paper.

Lesson: This morning I have something I want to show you. (A dust-laden object.) Do you know what we call this material that is on this (whatever your dusty object is)? ... Dust! What does your mother or father do with it? ... THEY WIPE IT AWAY. *(Clean off your object.)* Dust is always in the air around us. That is why we have little hairs in our nose so that the dust will be caught there and not enter our lungs. Since dust is always in the air, it will land on the surfaces around us and they will become very dusty unless someone takes the time to clean them off.

The dust reminds us of all the things that can mess life up. When something needs to be corrected or cleaned up or put away, someone has to do it or it will not get done. Can you imagine what a mess we would have here in church if every Sunday the people here just threw the bulletins on the floor and then no one picked them up during that week, and this happened week after week?

The same thing applies at home or out of doors. If we want things to look nice, if we want to be able to move about, we need to do our part to remove the "dust" of life. And you can help. When you see something that needs to be put away or picked up, do it. Don't expect someone else to take care of it. When each person does his or her part, we will all live in a cleaner, nicer church and home and world.

Now, as you go back to your family, see if you can remember what I have just said. *(Throw out pieces of paper to see if any of the children will pick them up.)*

Possible Times To Use This Illustration In The Home:
- When your child has failed to clean up after doing something messy.
- When you are housecleaning.
- When you are driving down a road where others have dumped garbage.

Scriptural Background: "The heavens are the Lord's heavens, but the earth he has given to the sons of men" (Psalm 115:16).

A Lesson From A Bouquet

Purpose: To see in a flower the greatness of God's creation and the wonder of our own individuality.

Material: A bouquet of flowers, either at the front of the church or one you brought with you.

Lesson: Today, I would like to play a guessing game with you. Here is the first clue. Almost every Sunday, when we gather here in our church, we all look upon something that is always different, yet it always has the same name. *(Modify this if you do not use flowers in your church.)* What is it? ...

(Second clue, if needed.) There are usually two of them (or whatever number of bouquets are usually displayed at the front of your church). What is it? ...

(Third clue, if needed.) They are made of flowers. What is it? ... A bouquet.

Every Sunday, we are reminded of the greatness of God's creation as we look at the beautiful flowers that he has formed. They come in all kinds of colors and shapes and sizes, and it is because of the different flowers that the bouquet is so beautiful.

There is a lesson for us here. Sometimes we get upset with others because they do something in a different way than what we would do it. Or they do not like the same things that we like. Or they dress in a different way. When other boys and girls do not want to do what you want to do, don't get angry with them. Just recognize that they are different and that is all right. God has made us all different and we need to be thankful for that difference and to see how it adds beauty to our shared lives.

(If you have access to a copy machine.) As a reminder of what we thought about today. I have a drawing of a bouquet that you can take home and color. Perhaps you can send it to your grandparents.

Possible Times To Use This Illustration In The Home:
- When you have a bouquet of flowers in your home, and you need to help your child understand the beauty of being different.
- When you have provided the flowers for your church's service of worship.
- When you have visited a florist or a greenhouse.

Scriptural Background: "Consider the lilies of the field, how they grow; they neither toil or spin; yet I tell you, even Solomon in all his glory was not arrayed like one of these" (Matthew 6:28, 29).

What Do You Do When You Get Hurt?

Purpose: To show children that we have a responsibility to do what we can to take care of ourselves. After we have done all we can, then we must leave the rest in God's hands.

Material: A box of bandage strips that contains the number you need to give one to each child.

Lesson: Have any of you ever hurt yourself? ... What happened? ... *(Let the children share their experiences.)* What did you do when you were hurt? ... Most of the time, when we are hurt, we use some medicine and maybe a bandage; and then we wait.

There are wonderful powers at work within us to help us get well again. For example, if you cut your finger, the blood forms a scab that prevents you from losing a lot of blood. You can help that process by protecting the wound and keeping it clean. But the healing will take place in your body simply because God created you that way.

So the lesson we learn from thinking about what happens when we get hurt is to do what we can to make things better and then we wait, for in time healing will take place.

As a reminder of this, I would like each one of you to take a bandage and give it to your mother or father who can carry it with them just in case you can get hurt sometime. They will then be prepared to do what they can to help you and then you can let God's power work in you.

Possible Times To Use This Illustration In The Home:
- When a child is hurt and needs a bandage.
- When a child has hurt feelings. Again, time is the great healer.
- When you want to help your child understand that we need to plan ahead.

Scriptural Background: "Bless the Lord, O my soul, and forget not all his benefits; who forgives all your iniquity, who heals all your diseases" (Psalm 103:2, 3).

A Good Deed Is Like A Candle

Purpose: To encourage children to do good things for other people.

Material: A candle and a jar. A dime for each child in individual envelopes.

Lesson: This is something that we see each week as we gather here and I am sure you know what it is. At the beginning of the worship service, we light the candles up front. *(At home, candles on the table could be used.)*

These candles stand for many things. For example, Jesus told us to let our light so shine before others that they may see the good things we do and then they will thank God for your goodness (Cf. Matthew 5:16).

There is an interesting thing about a candle that is burning. You must let the candle burn out in the open or it will go out. Let me show you what happens when you cover up the flame. *(Cover it with the glass jar.)*

To be a good person, you have to do good things. It is not good enough to just think about doing something nice for someone else. Others need to experience your goodness. It has to be done out in the open so that it can be experienced by the people around you.

Now, if you had a dime, can you think of something good you could do with it for others? ... *(Wait for the children to offer answers. If none are offered, share the following with them):* Place it in the collection plate to help support your church; buy a package of gum and share it with a friend; put ten cents with it and buy a post card and send a note to a friend or to your grandparents.

This envelope contains a dime and I want you to take it and think about doing something nice for someone, and then do what you have thought about.

Possible Times To Use This Illustration In The Home:
- When a child seems too selfish.
- When your child has received some money as a present and all he or she can think about is what to buy for self.
- When your child has found some money.

Scriptural Background: "A good name is to be chosen rather than great riches, and favor is better than silver or gold" (Proverbs 22:1).

Magic

Purpose: To help children understand that God is always with us even though we cannot see him.

Material: Make your own magic picture, using the special procedure.

Special Procedure: Instructions for making a magic picture:
1. Take an 8" X 8" piece of paper. On one side draw a fish. On the other side draw an underwater scene with seaweed and shells, etc.
2. Take a piece of cardboard and draw, paste, or trace your pictures on to it; one on each side. (Color if you desire.)
3. Punch two small holes (centered and one-half inch apart) on each side of the cardboard square.
4. Obtain two pieces of string, each about 18 inches long.
5. Thread the string through the two holes on one side and tie to make a loop.
6. Repeat on the other side.
7. Loop the string over two fingers, one end in each hand.
8. Spin the square and then pull gently on the loops; relax and pull again. Repeat as often as you want to see the picture. The fish should appear in the water.
9. Try making other pictures, like a bear on one side and a forest on the other. Have fun!

Lesson: What I want to show you today is a kind of magic picture. Here is a piece of cardboard with a picture on each side. Attached to the cardboard is a string and when you spin the cardboard, like this, there is magic. The fish is in the water. *(Or the girl is on the horse; or whatever picture you have produced.)* Now, of course, the picture does not move from one side to the other; it just looks that way.

This is sort of the way it is in life. We cannot see God, but we believe he is always with us. With our faith, which is like spinning the picture, we become aware of his presence. In order to be aware of God in our life, there are special things we need to do to maintain our faith. We worship, we pray, we study his word and we look for the signs of his love every day. When we do these things, we soon discover that God is with us, even though we may not really see him when we look at just one side of the picture. A strong faith helps us to know that God is a part of our lives.

Possible Times To Use This Illustration In The Home:
- When a child questions the reality of God.
- When a child is drawing or coloring pictures.
- When your child is looking for something to do. Use this special procedure and make a magic picture. Then talk about it.

Scriptural Background: "Draw near to God and he will draw near to you" (James 4:8).

Words And Actions

Purpose: To help children understand that our actions must support our words.

Material: A number of small bags of M & M's, or some other kind of special treat.

Note: This object lesson can be used on the Sunday when your church presents Bibles to your young people, or adapted to some other Sunday.

Lesson: A very pleasant thing happened to me recently. As I was leaving the church, a school bus went by and upon the bus was a boy about your age, who is a part of our church family, and as he went by he waved to me. That made me feel good. *(Adapt this event to something that happened in your own life when a young child said "hello" to you.)* He was saying hello by that wave, and the smile on his face told me that he knew me and he was glad to see me. You see, actions can speak to us like silent words, and they are very important.

Today, we had an action that says to our third graders that reading the Bible is important. As a church, we show it is important by buying a personal Bible for each one of you as you enter third grade. Actions and words need to go together and support one another.

For example, if I said I like you and want to do something to make you happy and then took out some little bags of

M & M's and DID NOT give you some, my actions would not support my words. But I want what I say to help me know what to do. Therefore, since I do like you all and want to be your friend, I will give you a little special treat this morning. *(Pass out small bags of M & M's.)*

Possible Times To Use This Illustration In The Home:
- When your child fails to follow through on verbal statements.
- When you want to give your child a treat.
- Whenever someone in the family has experienced an action that was contrary to someone's words.

Scriptural Background: "Not every one who says to me, 'Lord, Lord,' shall enter the kingdom of heaven, but he who does the will of my Father who is in heaven" (Matthew 7:21).

Learning Obedience

Purpose: To help children understand the purpose of obeying.

Material: No special material is needed.

Lesson: Do any of you have a dog? ... Does your dog do what it is told to do? ... Can it do any tricks? ... Well, let me tell you what happened one night with a dog named Dana. Dana belonged to a family who lived in Wisconsin. One day, Dana's family decided to take a long trip to Europe. They were to be gone over a month. Dana could not go with them, so Dana's family took her to Illinois to stay with the grandparents.

It was winter time. One night, while Dana was staying in Illinois, she ran away. The people with whom she was staying called for her to come back, but she disobeyed. They looked for her for several hours but could not find her. They were afraid that she might have tried to head for her home in Wisconsin. Finally, she did come back to her home in Illinois, but she had a cut on her face and her paws were very sore from all the ice and snow. She could have been saved from those injuries if she had just listened to the people who were taking care of her when they called her to come home, but she wanted to do things her own way.

One of the important things about learning to obey is that we have to believe that whoever is telling us what to do has our best interest in mind. You know this is so with your parents. And we all have to believe it is so with God.

Jesus said, "If you love me you will obey my commandments" (Cf. John 14:15). Love and obedience go together. That is an important lesson to learn.

Possible Times To Use This Illustration In The Home:
- When a child does not obey.
- When a new puppy comes to your home.
- When your children think you are being unfair when you tell them they cannot do something.

Scriptural Background: "And we are witnesses to these things, and so is the Holy Spirit whom God has given to those who obey him" (Acts 5:32).

What Does It Mean To Be Independent?

Purpose: To help children understand the nature of freedom as we live with other people.

Material: A tray containing a variety of small candy bars so that each child present can have one.

Lesson: Independence is a big word. What do you think it means? . . . (Self-governing, free from the influence of others, self-reliant. *If no one can give the appropriate answer, tell them.*) It means you are free to do what you want to do. But we are never really completely independent. We all are dependent upon others to supply most of the things we use in life.

One of the most important places to use your independence is in the choices you make in life. You do not have to choose what everyone is choosing unless it is what you want. But here again, we do not have complete freedom. Our choices are always limited.

Let me show you what I mean. I want you to line up with the littlest ones at the head of the line. Since the rule here states little ones first, you do not have a choice because your size is already set.

Now, on this tray there are a variety of little candy bars. You have the freedom to choose what you want, but we will start with the little ones first and so as the people before you choose, your choices will be limited by whatever is left.

We live in a land where we have freedom, but that does not mean we can always do just whatever we want to do. We live with other people and their freedom may affect what we can choose.

Now, as you go back to your seats, feel free to take a candy bar with you, starting with the smallest child.

Possible Times To Use This Illustration In The Home:
- Near Independence Day.
- When a child states, "That's not fair!" to help that child understand how conditions may influence what happens to him or her.
- When your child is trying to learn how to get along with other people in the house or in school.

Scriptural Background: "For freedom Christ has set us free; stand fast therefore, and do not submit again to a yoke of slavery" (Galatians 5:1).

Fun With Seeds

Purpose: To remind children about the importance of what they produce each day. Daily actions reveal each one's character.

Material: A package of seeds for each child.

Lesson: Do you know where seeds come from? . . . (From plants and trees.) When do they come? . . . (When the plant or tree is mature. Some seeds come in the spring and some in the fall.) And what happens to some of those seeds when they fall upon the ground? . . . (They start to grow.)

One of the most interesting things about seeds is that you get what you plant. In other words, if I plant an apple seed I will get an apple tree and that tree will produce apple seeds. If I plant corn seeds, I will get corn. And so it goes.

Seeds will always produce what they are supposed to produce. GOD HAS PLANNED IT THAT WAY. Jesus used this fact in one of the lessons he taught. He said, "You will know them by their fruit"; and the fruit of a tree is its seed (Cf. Matthew 7:16). What he meant by that was that a good person will do good things. Or to put it another way, if you want to be seen as a good person, then you have to do good things. It is a lesson we all need to remember.

This morning I have a package of seeds for each one of you. Plant them at home and see what you get from your seeds.

Possible Times To Use This Illustration In The Home:
- In the springtime or the fall, when seeds are seen in nature.
- To remind your child that, as members of the family, you all have special expectations of one another. When the child produces what is expected, it shows what kind of family he or she is from.
- When you want to stress the importance of personal character.

Scriptural Background: "If you love those who love you, what credit is that to you? For even sinners love those who love them. And if you do good to those who do good to you, what credit is that to you? For even sinners do the same. . . . But love your enemies, and do good . . . and you will be sons of the Most High; for he is kind to the ungrateful and the selfish" (Luke 6:32-36).

Why Remember Others*

Purpose: To help children think about the contribution of past generations.

Material: You might want to have a library book, a Bible and a hymnal on hand.

Lesson: Tomorrow is a national holiday. Do you know what it is called? ... (Memorial Day.) What is the purpose of Memorial Day? ... (Basically, a day to remember the people who died to keep our country free.) But it is also a good time to remember all the people who have helped us in the past.

It is important for us to remember others because other people are important to us. For example, we did not build this church building. People who lived before us provided for this church to be built. We should be thankful for what they did. We did not write the music we sing. We did not write or even print the Bible we read. Other people, who lived before us, provided these things for us.

Now, one way we have of saying "thank you" is to see that we take good care of what we have received from others, so that we can pass it on to other people. Have you ever taken out a book from the library? ... What do you do with it after you have read it? ... (Return it, in the same condition as when you received it so that others can use it.)

Taking care of what we have received from others is the best way for us to remember them and to show that we appreciate what they have done for us. So, when you use something, in your church or school or home, and it has been provided for you by someone else, take good care of it.

Possible Times To Use This Illustration In The Home:
- When a child has not been careful with something that belongs to someone else.
- When a child loans something to someone. Talk about what you expect from that other person.
- When the family has an occasion to remember past generations.

Scriptural Background: "I am reminded of your sincere faith, a faith that dwelt first in your grandmother Lois and your mother Eunice and now, I am sure, dwells in you" (2 Timothy 1:5).

*Use Memorial Day Sunday.

Take Time To Smell The Roses

Purpose: To stress the importance of taking time to appreciate what God has given to us in his created world.

Material: If possible, have a fresh fragrant rose on hand.

Special Procedure: This object lesson should be used when the weather is pleasant outside.

Lesson: Each Sunday, as we gather for worship, we have flowers at the front of the sanctuary, as you can see this morning. They are very pretty and remind us of the wonder of God's creation. *(At home, you can call attention to a flower garden.)*

Most of the time what many people do is just look at the flowers; and that is fine. But now and then, we find a flower — like the rose — that offers us more than just a beautiful sight. Do you know what else a rose offers? ... *(Let them smell the flower.)* ... A beautiful fragrance.

Sometimes we become so busy that we do not take time to enjoy the things we have around us. This morning we all came to church. Since it is a beautiful morning, we all should have stopped for a moment and inhaled the nice fresh air. Or we should have looked at the beautiful blue sky, or stopped for a moment to listen to the birds sing.

When you get home today after church and sit down for your meal at lunch, I hope you will take time to enjoy the meal and not just eat it as fast as you can because you have something else you want to do.

Sometimes we get so busy in life that we do not even take time to breathe deeply, and that is a shame. Let's do that right now. Take a deep breath and let it out slowly. *(Ask everyone to do it.)* Isn't life wonderful?

Possible Times To Use This Illustration In The Home:
- When the weather is changing to more pleasant temperatures.
- When you see roses, or other fragrant flowers, blooming in a garden.
- When your child seems to be too busy to do important things.

Scriptural Background: "I believe I shall see the goodness of the Lord in the land of the living! Wait for the Lord; be strong, and let your heart take courage; yea, wait for the Lord!" (Psalm 27:13, 14).

Index

Scripture References